THROUGH THE EYES OF LIFE

"An unique designer piece that only a daughter will own for a lifetime and above."

KITHMI GUNARATNE

authorHOUSE®

AuthorHouse™
1663 Liberty Drive
Bloomington, IN 47403
www.authorhouse.com
Phone: 833-262-8899

Published by AuthorHouse 12/30/2020

ISBN: 978-1-6655-1247-3 (sc)
ISBN: 978-1-6655-1246-6 (e)

Print information available on the last page.

Any people depicted in stock imagery provided by Getty Images are models, and such images are being used for illustrative purposes only. Certain stock imagery © Getty Images.

Illustration and photography by Kithmi Gunaratne.

This book is printed on acid-free paper.

To my beloved parents
who are a constant pillars of
strength, supporting me through all
my decisions.

To all my uncles, aunties and friends
who have supported, encouraged and
nurtured my writing career.

OPEN AND SHUT

A listener
Is called god
Because he or she has learnt the art of understanding
Not because he listens
But because not everyone puts themselves in the other
person's shoes
And gazes from the others' perspective

Life has those open and shut moments
And they will keep happening
Make sure you fall in love with the open and shut both
Because your lover has to be the one who has been with you
when life shuts you out and opens you up

Today or tomorrow you will find the one person
But not everyone will
And yet if you keep waiting
In the most unexpected of moments
You will find the love of your life

Not only for today
But for today, tomorrow and forever
Love is your heartbeat that has to be beating with your lover
until the nib
For the rest of your life
In all those open and shut moments
For all the aye times.

NEVER SAY GOODBYE

The wind of imperturbation is blowing
In this dawn of the night
Shimmering and twirling, the moon
Like a baby in her mother's arms

Sometimes between these long walks I wonder
The mysteries of love and life
My silence is distressed
Footsteps arising

A stranger
Someone to who everyone is asked not to speak
Yet pouring your heart out feels easier
I look at the watch
Twelve o'clock it struck

Just me and him in this dead of a night
Sitting in a train station
Me awaiting my train
I look at his face

Queries tossing through my head
A man alone at this time
I look at his face
A lack of fulfillment is manifested

The horn blows
My ride is here
I speak out for the first time
"Goodbye," I say
He replies," Never say Goodbye"
I look back
He is gone and so is the train.

CAN I EVEN FALL IN LOVE WITH MYSELF?

My mind spinning and thundering
Burning inside me
Hunger strikes like the dead man's shock
The pain of ignorance and of poverty
Together between my arms

Fighting to live today
How could I even dream of tomorrow?
Not even knowing if I'll see the sun rising between the morning clouds
How could a child like me even dream to be in the busy streets?

Fights of the boxing ring rising through my heart of pain
How can these people be so ignorant?
Vehicles on the streets, people on the pavements
Am l that unnoticeable?
What can you expect me to think?

If the future I see is thus colorless
Do I want to live in a world this cloudy?
With humans without feelings
How can I even fall in love with myself?

LOVE THAT NEVER DIES

Spectators around with all eyes on your face
Victory or defeat
There's only one shoulder to rest
The lights of the day
In the hearts of our parents
Your soul can rest in victory or defeat

In this race to be great
We lose the meaning to live our life
Why be the pawn to the road of race?
When you and I can win as one

The morning star and the evening star
All in one
One blessed soul will have the best in pair
Parents are the blessing of heaven
With love that ebbs like the waters of paradise

But one mistake can lead to the whole of hell
All that is with the future in mind
With love and hope
That you will be one good child

To trust and care
With no return gifts in mind
All they do is love and wait
Forever and forever until bygone times are written again

When can their glory fade for the great deeds they've done.
With no expectation in heart
But just a hope in mind
That one fine day we will love them again.

READING AND WRITING

Crushed papers
And dried up ink
Failed attempts lying around
Messy desks and dirty floors

Empty cups and piles of reread books
Reading and writing has become a practice
The red eyes and the sulky face
Sleepless nights and a heavy head
With thoughts in mind
But no time in hand

Coffee again and books again
Same routine day and night
Not stepped out in days to see
Reading and writing
Has become the story

Until all the tiredness becomes worthy
When at last your books make history
Watching those smiling faces
I read and write
Again and again
Only to see those smiles again.

STORIES OF LIFE

Bounded by stories
And living a story
We are all stories in this book of life
Everyone has their own but only some design it

The others just be the ordinary story
Today and forever
Our clock stops any minute from now
Then we lose time to color our story

The difference between time and us
Is that no matter what, time keeps on going but
We keep waiting till
Unknowingly everything has left
And our journey of life ends without a purpose

So as the famous words say,
Don't count the days, make the days count
But the question is do we do this
If we are honest it's a no
But we just keep nodding and let the words swing by

Change now or never
Because life is not our call
We may be shaping our surroundings
Our mother, father, wife or child
But life is not at our beck and call
It is at its own.

ONE LAST CHANCE

Step by step as the day melts into dusk
More or ever the counted minutes have gone away
Looking back and asking yourself
Have you lived your best today?

Today or tomorrow
Now or then
We cannot say what the world awaits
All we can see is the clock ticking by

Ask yourself again and again have you lived your best today
Yes, or no
No one else cares
But please again, go again and live again
Because bygone times cannot be brought again
You can only see the now and present

Clear your eyes and look again
Rewrite history and rewrite your story
Once again for one last time
Live life again
Because everyone deserves one last chance.

AN EAGLE ALIVE

The dark side of everything
Is what the eye prays for
Clasping on it, whaling through it
What other opportunities are there?

You can never be good in the hearts of others
Why do we try to impress the illegitimate other's?
The heart of yours, the soul that we thrive in
Is only a blessing
For the one with the eyes of an eagle

Grieving through it, mourning through it
Is the call of God
But rise again and stand again
Because we get only one true life

Shove the bad swivel the good
Live the best in this so-called life
You get only one and one final call
Prove to yourself that you're an eagle alive.

SMALL FEELINGS

A man in the kitchen
In the dead of the night
With the smell of the traditional *"Achcharu"*
All the childhood memories flashing again

The small feelings evoked again
All the memories brought back to life
To the last time he had his mother's homemade *"Achcharu"*

Can't go back
He looks around
The same smell, the same taste
He felt as if he lived his childhood again
As he walked away, whispering to himself
"Anthimata ithuru wenne jeewithey vIndhapu dheval vitharai"

TRUE LOVER'S HEART

Tangling fires in the clouds of eyes
Rushing waters through the thunderstorm lives
Raising and shoving for the time to come
What can you call it?
The true lover's heart

The stomach all crawling
With the nerves hanging out
Drooling in love and loosing on track
Love is the mystery
That we all fight for

Pains of love and the cries of joy
All the emotions under one hungry plate
It breaks you and mends you
Has everything to gain and to lose

What do you see the love or hate?
In this circle of life
Do you see it with eyes of hatred?
Or the eyes of love-
Because the tangling fire has some time to wait
Until you find the true lover's heart.

IT'S NOT
THE SAME

It's not the same
Nothing is the same
Until you look into the eyes
And when you do
It changes my present as well as the future

My day and night change places
My heart yearns for you
We seem far yet so close
I know that when I need you the most
You will be right next to me

I also know that you will bring me the sun and the moon
That's what makes you so special
You are there for me
Not when I need you
But also when I don't need you

You are there everywhere
We will meet again
If not now surely later
This is all we've brought
But it's not the end
Our legacy will go on forever
And the world will look at you in the same way
I looked at you.

WORTH THE WAIT

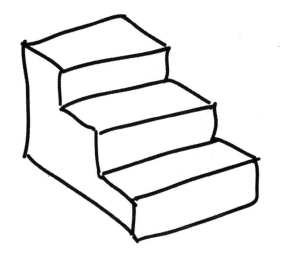

Step by step
I start believing in you
The more I do, the deeper I fall
Unknowingly I have lost myself in your stories
And again the more and more you play your stories
I keep falling and falling
Into your trap of love

You played with my heart
And left me lying here
I cry in pain every day
There is not even a moment that I don't miss you
But when I see you walk away
I feel so angry
And yet my love for you is stronger than my pain

I've dreamt the many stories
That we would tell our children
Now our children have become my children
No more our stories but my stories
I promise I didn't wish for this to happen
But you broke us
And now there is nothing left

Through this I realized today
That God had better plans for me
Now that I have fallen in love again
I give love another chance to sweep me away
Today I see love is much bigger than anything you gave me
But always and forever I will be wishing you well
Because you taught me that love hurts but it's worth the
wait.

YOU WILL ALWAYS BE MY HERO

The sound of nature would wake me up
But now the steps of your feet moving across
Give me the wake-up call
Then you kiss my forehead
Making my day so gradient

Every time you held me close
It felt beyond eternity
Each time I fell asleep on your shoulders
Those were the best slept nights

Fifteen years and still counting
I see so many pictures
Of us growing old together
All those letters you wrote to me
While we were young
I will cherish them until my last breath and also after
The days of youth gone
But the old yet to come

They say old is gold
I see now why they all did say so:
Underneath they were all great lovers
Old or young you will always be my hero
Baby you are my hero forever
Even after we've become stardust
I will love you even through the stars

THE BRIGHTEST STAR

Staring at all those stars at night
Floating through the river banks
With just a paddle in hand and the stars above
I float alone lost in my thoughts

Letting out all those stories engraved in my heart
I take my journal and write to you
I know you won't respond this time
But when we meet again I know you will answer all my letters
And many more

You will tell me the stories
That you heard
When you were entangled in the arms of God
I come here every night and write you a letter
Looking up at the stars I see you shining bright
Smiling through the glittering stars
You are the brightest star down here
Baby you loved everything about everyone
Looking back now
Again and again I keep falling in love with you
All over again.

THE SECRET
OF NATURE

The first time you close your eyes
Just hoping that you won't die
But once you do it
You want it more and more

Deep dark blue
Waves that hit your skin
You're floating underwater
For the first time
Your feeling so happy
In between the waters tiny fish cut through

Breathtaking corals
The sacred universe you never knew existed
The holy palace underneath the universe
It fulfils your soul in peace

The fear you had the first time you jumped
Has now disappeared
And now passion has taken over
Dark blue, then light blue
The colors keep changing as you dive deeper
The fish swimming like little light bulbs
That light up the water

The feeling is magical
It makes you fall in love with nature
All over again
The feeling the water can bring you
Is priceless
And beyond imaginable
This is the secret that nature has
For the one who explores.

TICKLES OF LOVE

When your skin is so rough
And when your face is full of freckles
I will still kiss your forehead
Because baby you will never outgrow my arms

Somewhere between the stars and the moons
We've met before
The love that I carry is from the past
Our children will know the story of our love
And they will carry the same essence you had
The first time you swept me off my feet

The lingering feeling
When you're next to me
Tickles my heart in and out
Floating and swimming in the pond you've made
The one that we call our tiny home
Is filled with memories of you and I
My love, I will love you till the end of time.

LIFE

Life we call it
But do we really know what life is?
Different people have different perspectives
Yours from mine and mine from yours

I wonder
Again and again
Searching for this meaning of life
You're born and then you fall in love
And then again
Few years later
You go leaving everything and everyone behind

So why are you born?
Because you have to live
Live in the moment
Learn new things
Seek adventures
Find your own path
Make your own mistakes
Learn from them
And set off on the adventure again

This is that so called life
It takes us in circles
But our target Is right in front of us
If you miss it
It's gone

I don't know about you
But me
I am treasuring each minute
And making memories
Cause I know we get only one
At least the only one you'll know about.

UNCONDITIONAL
LOVE

The sky so dark
Still carries pride
Because even this darkness has beauty inside
If you are willing to shine

Stars are bright
And the sky so clear
They never fail to entangle us
Night or morning
Both have wonder
No reason why
But they just have

Not like you or any of us
The moons so true
That respect, is all you see
In full or half
It always arrives

He keeps his promise
No matter what
No one can be
Anything like him

He is just full of passion
To pay his children a friendly surprise
Just like a father's
Unconditional love.

STILL I'LL BE WAITING

You say you know me
But if you did
You would have known
What I went through behind my eyes

You know I don't like those sugar coated lines
Yet I keep falling over again
It hurts when people go away
But it hurts even more
When the people so close
Feel so far

I don't know how or why we've got here
But still I'll be waiting
Until you notice
Because I am not used to anything
Without you

We stay so close
But still you can't see the pain in my eyes
You kiss my forehead and go away
And still you see no difference in me

I don't know how or why we've got here
But I'll keep waiting until you notice
Because I'm not used to life without you.

HIGH UP THERE

You rose so early
Behaved so strangely
Sitting so close I couldn't understand
What happened?

Maybe if I did
You would have stayed longer
I'm so sorry I couldn't see your trauma
But no matter what, you were a star in my heart

When you left me here
With nothing to hope
My heart bled so much
That I couldn't feel a thing
For a long time

It took me so long
To stop blaming myself
Because all I could see was my guilty hands
But when I made peace with myself
I saw you smile
From high up there
Then I realized
That I had peace
From both the sides.

IF WE LOSE

I don't roar out loud
Thinking of you
But nothing matters
Because you don't care

How can I stop caring?
Because you're everything I know
I don't know anything
Besides you

You still don't see or either don't care
About the love that I give you
I don't care
Because I will keep loving you
All my life

I'm trying my best to give you the best
Because I don't want our children
To know that their parents
Lost the battle of love

If we lose
We make them lose their hope
To fall in love
And to paddle in this boat
To find their home.

THE RIGHTEOUS ONES

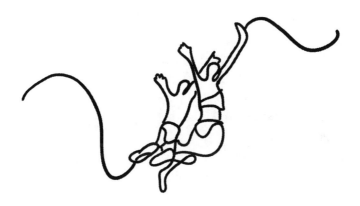

Life is hard
And I know it too
But we chose to swim it through
Because God gave us his courage

Now that I'm here
There is no turning back
Because I am a fighter
And so is my father

Everything is hard
Because in life there is no easy way out
But that is what makes this journey
Hard it is but once you get through it
You see pure paradise
And you realize why God sent you

It is a blessing to a have a life
To see the wonders and taste the delights
If you do it right
You will have it right
Because God makes no mistakes
For the righteous ones.

SET MY SOUL
ON FIRE

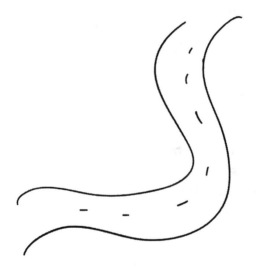

You brought me here
So now I am here
I see the world through my eyes
And not yours

You want something different
But so do I
We can be separated
Yet united
But you seem to not understand
You and I are not one, but two

You brought me here
But I want a different path
I see the world through my eyes
And not yours

I don't know why?
But I want to pursue freedom
That life has
While you want to dominate
I want to set my soul on fire

You wont get me now
Maybe never
But don't worry
I will wait until you understand.

YOU WILL ALWAYS BE MY BABY IN HAND

You were so soft
That even the slightest noise
Would give you a shiver
Now when I see you so big
Conquering these fears
I feel so proud

The little baby I had known for those long years
Has suddenly become a man overnight
You took so much pride
In everything you did
Now that you have left before me
I have nothing to say
But goodbye

I wish you well
In everything you do
Wait for me, wherever you are
Until we meet again
Because you will always be my
Baby in hand

BALANCE

Everyone seems so close
Yet so far
Even our families have secrets
That are tied in their tongues
Not to be let out

Some people don't have feelings
And some understand more
Too much is bad and so is less
Moderation
We call it
But who does this
Everyone wants everything

Either you are too fast or too slow
If you lose the balance you're left behind
Everyone has their own forte
But the one who seeks it is the real winner
Everyone can earn
But respecting what you do is something
Only a few can do

Some people who are close
Are so far away
Because everything needs to be felt
And when you don't feel it
The passion inside you dies

Mostly you don't let your feelings out because your ego lies
with pride
But the problem is when you don't
The train has already left

And it's too late
Do what you have to
Say what you want to
Because otherwise you're left with
Only regret
And regret slowly and steadily kills you inside.

WITLESS MIND

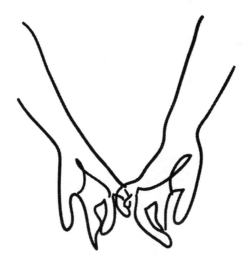

I let you go
When I wanted you to stay
I trapped my feelings hoping you would dig them out
My ego was stronger than my love for you
Now I have no words
To express my feelings
I failed you in my vows

You were my moon and sun
Now I know that I am too late
When I see you entangled in his hand
I reminisce the good old days
When we were together

My witless mind fooled me again
Into letting you go
Because I thought you would come running back to me
My hopes were so high and so was my pride

I have lost my race today
I'm lost without you in my life
I have no purpose to wake up to now
Because I only woke up to see you smile

This time you couldn't be mine
But next time I promise
I will be better
A soul that deserves you in and out.

THE DESIGNER PIECE

No matter what
He is always by your side
Supporting you through thick and thin
He is slightly distinct from the flock
But he is your silent supporter and strength

The first man every daughter comes across
No one can love, just the way he does
He taught her to fly with no boundaries
And treats her like a queen

He is always smiling
Even when life throws thorns along his path
He is like a ray that warms you up
And he leaves a footprint in the middle of your heart
With his warm words and kind thoughts

God has designed
A personal empirical for every daughter
Because he can't come
In person to check
He has made an emperor of love
He brings out the warrior in every girl
Carving a path for his angel to float in

There is no other like him
On earth or above
A unique designer piece
That only a daughter will own
For a lifetime and above.

NOT YOUR FAULT

Some people will not hear you
Because they haven't dug deep enough into their hearts
They are surrounded by the noise of the others
So when you speak wise
They shall not hear
It's not your fault
But theirs

They are not fortunate enough
To latch your words
They make you insecure
Not because you are bad
But because they are jealous of your triumph

They will not hear
However much you try
So just don't bother
To be heard by them
They are not worthy of your words
But only of the false alarms.

LOOK BACK
AND SMILE

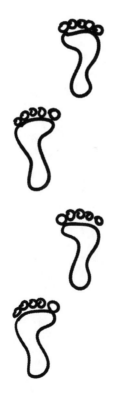

It does hurt
My body shivers
Feels like my head's going to explode
But I still wake up and keep going

Because my dedication is more salient
Than my pain
It liberates me
It opens up a wide space for me to roam free

Nothing matters
Because my final goal
Is to be the best version of myself
I don't want to win
And be honored
But I want a fulfillment from within

I want to leave my footprints
On these steps
So that when I am old
I can look back and smile.

NEVER GIVE UP

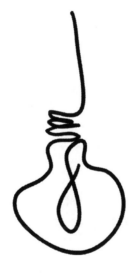

It hurts so much
Believe me or not
It feels so numb
I look up at the clock
But it just does not move

I don't want to wake up
But it just doesn't happen
Some way or the other
The light hits in

I shut myself in
Draw all the blinds down
Yet the light creeps in
I don't know why you left me alone
And you were my brightest star

You shone so bright
Baby you were the brightest star
Now nothing feels the same
Without you in it
But I won't give up
Because you wouldn't have wanted to see me fail

I will rise again
Stronger than before
But it will take some time
To get back on my feet
But I promise
To never give up
Because you taught me that it gets better.

THE INCOMPLETE STORY

You blamed me for not loving you
And dumped me like in a garbage dump
You claimed that I never said 'I love you'
You were so naïve that you didn't notice
That I had said I loved you many more times

It was only different from the ordinary way
I didn't use the three little words
But every time I baked you your favorite cake
And every time I held your hand and walked paths
Every time I waited down the stairs without a complaint
even after half an hour
Waiting for you to come down
That was my love, for you

But you were so insensitive
That you searched for three little words
When all this time, all I did was say 'I love you'
You didn't notice the fleeting moments we shared
Because you were too busy looking for words
When I had completely lost myself at unveiling
My love

You didn't notice
All the things I did just to see you smile
All my efforts had been in vain
Because you dumped me one night like garbage
My story of love will live incomplete
For a man who had never seen my toils.

SMILE

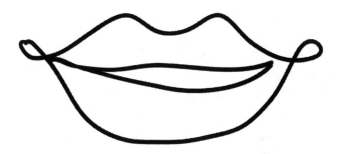

Smile, my dear, smile
Because there will come a day where you will
Regret all those days you hadn't smiled
I promise to you not every day will be bad
But there will be some days that you mourn

I promise it will not last forever
Because it doesn't rain everyday
The sun shall shine one day
And spread its essence
Through your darkness

When it does happen
You will be smiling once again
Just because it's gloomy now
Don't stop smiling
Because the one who wins
Always smiles even through darkness

That's the power
You have to gain
My dear you shine the most
Amongst all these broken souls.

GOODBYE KISS

Deep down you knew
She was never going to stay
Yet you gave her everything you had
Your heart was so warm
And full of pride for the woman you had
For at least sometime

But she just left
With no gratitude just attitude
Even then all you did was leave her wild
When we asked you
Why so soft?
All you said was
She was too big, to fit in my soul

And you said
She was never mine
And was never meant to be mine
But I lived my best
For the little days she could be mine

She was a broken soul
With a broken heart
All I did was try to fix this broken soul
With my love

But it was just not her way
So she left
Without even
One last Goodbye kiss.

OUR BABY GIRL

I painted every inch
With showers of love
Pink and white
Just the way
You had wanted to see your baby girl

You loved her so dearly
But left too early
The karma had come even before
She could move

I don't know whose karma it was
Was it ours or our baby girls'
She never saw you
And neither did you get to hold her
Oh my love
What do I say
To this little soul

She wouldn't want to bear the pain
To know that her father had left long ago
Without even saying goodbye
How can I tell her that he had become stardust?
Long before she had even come

But don't worry my love
I will tell her all the stories you wanted to share
She will know how much of a great father
You would have been

I will tell our baby
That her father shines bright

Amongst the stars
Watching over his baby girl
A twinkling star
Smiling alone
And laughing out loud
Each time he sees her reach new heights.

FLY TOGETHER

You sat with me
And hugged me tight
You kept silent
Even when I grumbled all those nights

All those sleepless nights you spent
Just to put me to sleep
Now your baby has finally outgrown the nest
With wings to fly
Up high above

Now it's my turn to see you fly
You spent your youth
Raising me

Now you've grown so old
And I'm flying so high
But now I will rest
And come down again
And smile with you
And laugh with you
And tomorrow we will fly together.

DROWNED IN THE WORDS

We both drowned in the words
Neither one of us were saying
Seems like the external noise was stronger
Than our love

We had slowly drifted apart
And had let the world decide for us
Gradually it killed the both of us
And the spark had left long ago
And today we stand divided

For the noise that wasn't ours
We let go of ourselves
And watched our souls rip apart
We sat there and did nothing but watch
And today we sit and mourn this loss

Maybe if we had trusted ourselves
A little better than we have done
Today we would have a little story to tell
For the ones who had asked for the story
Of our love.

ONLY A PHASE

You think it is easy
But it is not
No one said love comes in easy
it is a process

You must learn to love
But not hold on too tight
Because when you press too hard
The bird flies away
Cause they find no joy in this nest

A time comes when love heals it all
But also comes a day where you must let go
Because that is what love is all about
If you really loved him
You would let him go

Because until you let go
You wouldn't find peace
Because deep down you know
That he wasn't happy
It's not your fault
But you were just not meant to be his
It was only a phase.

ONE STRONG
WOMAN

You broke me
And put me down
Hoping I wouldn't survive
But you forgot that I had lived long before
Without you

You left me with an unwritten story
It did hurt a bit
But don't think I can't survive
Because I will
I will rise
And will rise again
With a stronger face
And roar aloud

Then you shall hear my voice
One of a stronger woman
With a lion's strength
And a Queen's pride
I will rise
And will rise again
With a better version of myself

I don't need you, to survive
Because I had lived alone
Long before you had even crossed my path
So don't think I am one lame woman
Like the ones you had seen before

When time goes by
You will hear my story
Of one strong woman
Who had conquered the odds.

GO AWAY
SOCIETY

They tell you: don't do that
It's not good
Be this or that when your older
Because that is what gives you respect

The constant race to become either a doctor or engineer or
whatever
That's all the society bears
occupations for all those children born

Why so small
The mind of yours
What happens to the ones
With better creative minds?
Not everyone would want to be that

You teach the children to be what society wants
But not follow their hearts
Why don't we teach our kids to find themselves?
What in this process of life
Why can't we hope for a happy child?
But no they don't want it
All they want is doctors or engineers
Just to be able to pay the bills

Why do you torture our little ones?
Don't they deserve a little peace of mind?
To run and play
According to their little dreams
Without the boundaries
Drawn by you or I.

MY BABY DOLL

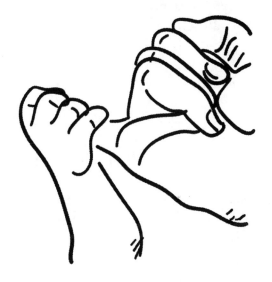

The first time your tiny fingers caught mine
You held on so tight
With all your strength
You giggled so much
And talked in a gibberish language

You have an entire life ahead of you, my child
Dream my baby doll
You have everything to mix, crack and test
Set on all the adventures
And learn from the trials

You talked so much
And cried very little
You were one happy baby
Your skin was so tender
And overwhelmed my heart each time you smiled

My baby doll
I will walk you through all the walks of life
I will take you on my back
To see the wonders
Until you can do it alone

My little angel close your eyes
And paint your dreams
And when you reach them
Let them fly
Then hop and run and find another
Because the world awaits you
To bring your new dreams to life.

HEARTBEAT

The heartbeat that keeps thrashing
The beat of my country
Makings steps ahead
The sound of her footsteps ringing in my ears

The mountains from paradise
And the waterfalls that ebb
We've had black days and red days
We've seen milestones of courage
And the hard work of our men
Who were raised by our *'lankamatha'*

We have sunsets and rainfall
Soil and water
The god destined nation
With many trees to bear fruit
But wounded people
With these treacherous of politics

Deep cuts in the souls
That cannot be healed
With no courage left to fight the system
They lie still under sun
Until they drift into their salvation

The sons they have lost
The husbands they have lost
Thirty years now but the country is bleeding
Because of the matches played
By the executors of law

'*Lankamatha*' we call out
The nation in which the mother roars
No color or race can change this mother
Who loves all her children in spite of their differences
She has raised millions of children
Who have brought her pride
But some have not

No matter the critics she kept going
Nurturing the daughters and sons
With her only motto in mind
'*Ratata nayanathi puthun vadamu.*'

POWER

I know I have been judged by many
For the way that I have conducted myself
But that is not going to change
Any of my ways
Because it is me
And I prefer to be myself

I won't let your words break me
Because people are always going to talk
No matter what?
And I am at no power to stop the small talk
And I'm not going to try
And please the illegitimate others

You keep talking
And gossiping
Because your words mean nothing to me
You are you and I am me
You can't change
Because my power lies within me.

MATCH MADE IN PARADISE

Like the sun and the moon
You lit up my world
Leaving footprints all over my heart
My heart is so full now
That I don't need anything anymore
Because I have you by my side

You stroke my head
With your tender fingers
And all my worries fade away
I fall asleep on your shoulder
And that's where I sleep the best

My love
You are the best
And we are a match made in paradise
You love has healed and nurtured me
In many different ways

The love you have shown me
Has taught me that life offers the best
You have taught me to live with no worries
And taught me that life can brush all the pain away
I wouldn't have known what life is like
Because you showed me a different path
Different from the one I had seen before.

INAMORATA

Perfect yet imperfect
Nothing seems surreal here
You wish but it's not
Fortunate or unfortunate
It is unknown

You are so lost
In your own world
Self-obsessed people would say
I guess that is what it is called

You are not
What I used to know
So much change
In such a short stubby time

You've lost yourself
My dear
And in return
Now you are breaking hearts

You say you have fallen in love
But for one inamorata
You have broken thousands more
Why so dramatic
In this surreal world
Balance yourself
That's what you've got to learn.

MAGICAL BABY

She came to us
Like an angel from paradise
She was everything we had dreamed of
Tiny little fingers
And tiny footsteps
That would make our heart melt very moment

Her pink chubby cheeks
She was such a delightful baby
She was so soft right from the beginning
She was a magical being

Her understanding for her age
She was beyond our imagination
She couldn't speak
But her actions so kind
She would kiss the screen
When tears rolled down the cartoon cheek

She was a magic able baby
We couldn't be any happy
For our little home
With a baby this delightful
We have a complete package
With thou spirit.

SENSITIVE SOULS

You have so much inside of you
Too real to be written through poems
And too old to be captured by photographs
You have so much beauty
Buried inside of you

You have a legacy
That runs through your blood
You have a unique story to say
If you worry
It has already been said

Don't worry
Because it hasn't been said by you
You have so much inside of you
Realistic captures of life
But they could be too old to be loved by everyone
It will be loved very deeply
By a few very heartily souls.

REGRET

He stood so brace
Staring at the portrait each day
His wife had left tis time
But he hadn't been there
To bid farewell

He loved her so solemnly
Treated her like a bibelot
With care and pride
She was one majestic piece of art

Now that old age has taken
His regrets are high
He sits reminiscing the good old days he shared with his
beloved
He had been too busy
Late in her life
That he had no time
To spare for the soul that they shared

Slowly and silently
The regret is now
Eating him up
As he sits watching the portrait
Of the woman whose life he had
Once had.

GAME OF CHESS

One piece at a time
Slowly and silently
Piece by piece
Mentally we plan
Until the plot takes a twist

The pawn goes first
Unleashing the barrier
Step by step
Bishops and knights take the move
Until the periphery
The woman in solitude doesn't make an entry

Silently and tactfully
She stands
Protecting her husband and her kingdom
This is what we see
Even in a game of chess
The power of a woman
And her poise.

SEARCH

I searched for you
When you didn't show up
I waited and waited
For you to arrive

Until at last
I lost powers
To convince Them
That you would come

That night my ancestors' power
Stood beyond my words could ever
Reluctantly I had to walk their path
They tied me with the other hand
Even that last moment
I waited and searched for you
In between the crowds
Before I stepped my foot onto that nuptial

I hoped and prayed
That you would appear
In between the crowds
But you didn't
So I had to leave us in the past
And set my foot into the future
In his hands.

A STORY TO TELL

You sat there but did nothing
When he told me all those things
You were watching
But did nothing to protect me
That moment I realized
That the man that I had all my life
Was not going to stand for me

But why my love
What haven't I done for you
For what makes it so difficult
For you to take the stand
For me

Why can't you at least
Pretend to defend me
To not fail my heart
At least for sometime
Hold on to me
Until I can process
What went wrong?

Don't worry my love
I will let you go
But please don't leave just yet
Because I have a story to tell.

THE TRAP

I didn't know if it was true
But believed in the little talk
Of the illegitimate
I didn't trust you well
When all you had tried was to
Wish me well

I was incautious
And believed everything
Everyone said
Today I am paying for my downfall
Because I hadn't trusted a man
Who had loved me this well

I look for you
Through the crowds
I look for you in the busy streets
I don't know how it has been for you
But all I do is spend my days
Looking for you

If you ever see me
Please come to me
Because I have a lot to say
I know I don't deserve a heart like yours
But you are a man
With one big heart

Now I am entangled
In the trap
Of my own mistakes.

"Life is like a puzzle and you have to keep looking for the little pieces to fit. When it fits keep smiling and when it doesn't try again because life is too short to worry about the little mistakes."

ABOUT THE AUTHOR

Kithmi Gunaratne is a young author born and raised in the city of Colombo, in the beautiful island of Sri Lanka surrounded by the ocean. She considers her faith and family to be most important to her. From a very young age she was encouraged to look at life differently by her father. She has portrayed her unique and different style of sighting at the world through her first collection of poetry "Through the eyes of life." The young author is also passionate about photography and drawing. She was exposed to both these crafts by her mother who was an enthusiast about art and photography. She believes that one should always do what makes them the happiest and that you only need a little light to make the world a better place which comes when you change the way you gaze at the world. Today, as a young author she hopes that her writing would impact the lives of others.

Printed in the United States
By Bookmasters